BEGINNING

BARITONE
UKULELE FINGERSTYLE

UKELIKETHEPROS

© 2023 TERRY CARTER

UKE LIKE THE PROS

CONTENTS

ISBN-13: **978-1-7359692-7-5**

Copyright 2023

TERRY CARTER

UKELIKETHEPROS.COM

DESIGNED BY M. @mapcontents

THE ESSENTIALS

It is important to learn and memorize these terms and symbols
because they not only apply to Ukulele but to all music.

Treble Clef or 'G' Clef   Staff

Time Signature

Measure Numbers   Measure or Bar   Bar Line   End

Top Number:
How Many Beats Per Measure

♩ = 120   Tempo Marks
120 bpm (beats per minute)

Repeat Sign

Bottom Number:
What Kind of Note Gets the Beat

Common Time:
Same as 4/4 Time

Notes On The Staff: There are seven notes in music (A. B. C. D. E. F. G) and they move
up and down alphabetically on the staff.

G   A   B   C   D   E   F   G   A   B   C   D   E   F   G   A   B   C   D   E   F

How To Remember The Notes:

Notes On The Lines   Notes In The Spaces

E (every)   G (good)   B (boy)   D (does)   F (fine)   F   A   C   E

HOW TO READ TAB

Tablature (TAB) is a form of music reading for the baritone ukulele that uses a 4 line staff and numbers. Each line of the staff represents a string on the baritone and the numbers represent which fret you play on. When looking at the TAB staff it reads like it's upside down on the paper compared to the strings of your baritone. On the TAB staff, the highest line (closest to the sky) represents the 1st string (E string) of the baritone, while the lowest line (closest to the ground) represents the 4th string (D string) of the baritone. When you see 2 or more notes stacked on top of each other on the TAB staff, that means you play those notes at the same time, like a chord.

BARITONE STRINGS

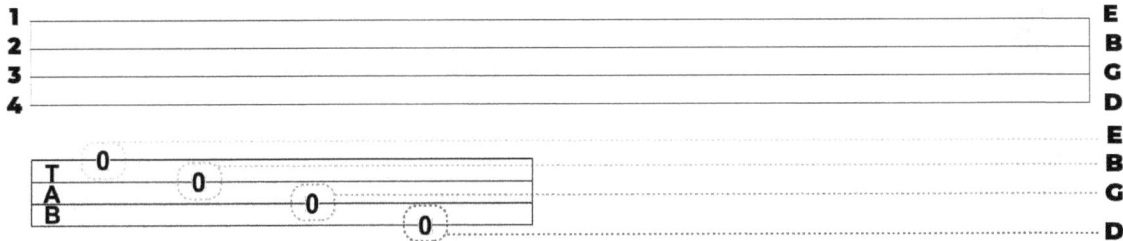

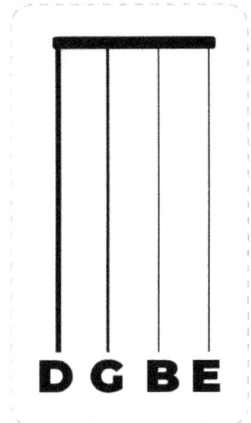

1rst STRING EXAMPLES

1.) E string. FIRST FRET.
2.) E string. THIRD FRET.
3.) E string. FIFTH FRET.

2nd STRING - B string. THIRD FRET.

3rd STRING - G string. SECOND FRET.

4th STRING - D string. SIXTH FRET.

CHORD

ARPEGGIO
USING THE G CHORD

PINCH
USING THE G CHORD

BARITONE PARTS

HEADSTOCK

ULTP SIGNATURE

STRINGS

NUT

TUNERS

FRETS

FRET MARKERS
ON FRETBOARD

SIDE DOTS

NECK

SIDE

ROSETTE

SOUND HOLE

HEEL

BINDING

SADDLE

SIDE

TOP

BRIDGE

BACK

BUTT

BARITONE HANDS

When playing fingerstyle on your baritone ukulele, you will see both letters and numbers to indicate which fingers to use both for your picking hand and your fretting hand. These letters and numbers will show up in the music notation, TAB, and/or chord diagrams.

FRETTING HAND	PICKING HAND
The left hand for right-handed players. will be indicated in the music or chord diagrams by numbers:	The right hand for right-handed players. will be indicated in the music by letters:
1=Index finger **3**=Ring finger **2**=Middle finger **4**=Pinky finger	**p**=Thumb **m**= Middle **i**=Index **a**= Ring **c**=pinky (not used in this course)

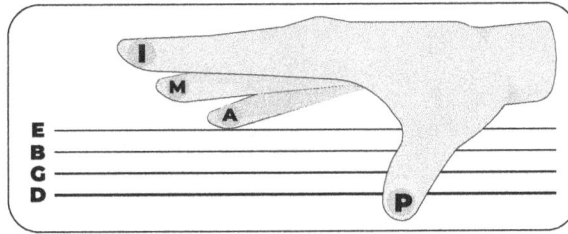

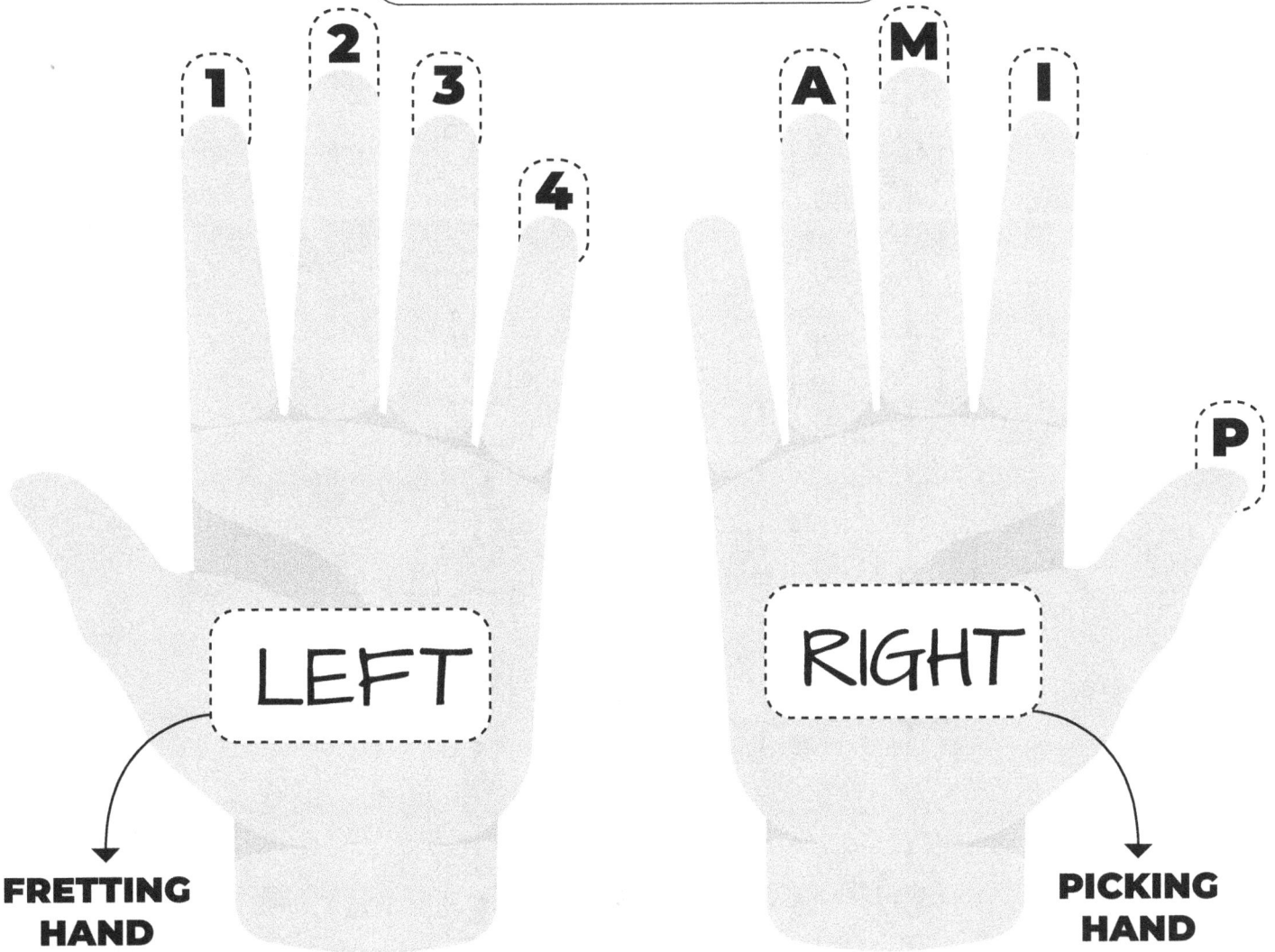

LEFT

FRETTING HAND

RIGHT

PICKING HAND

NOTES ON THE BARITONE UKULELE NECK

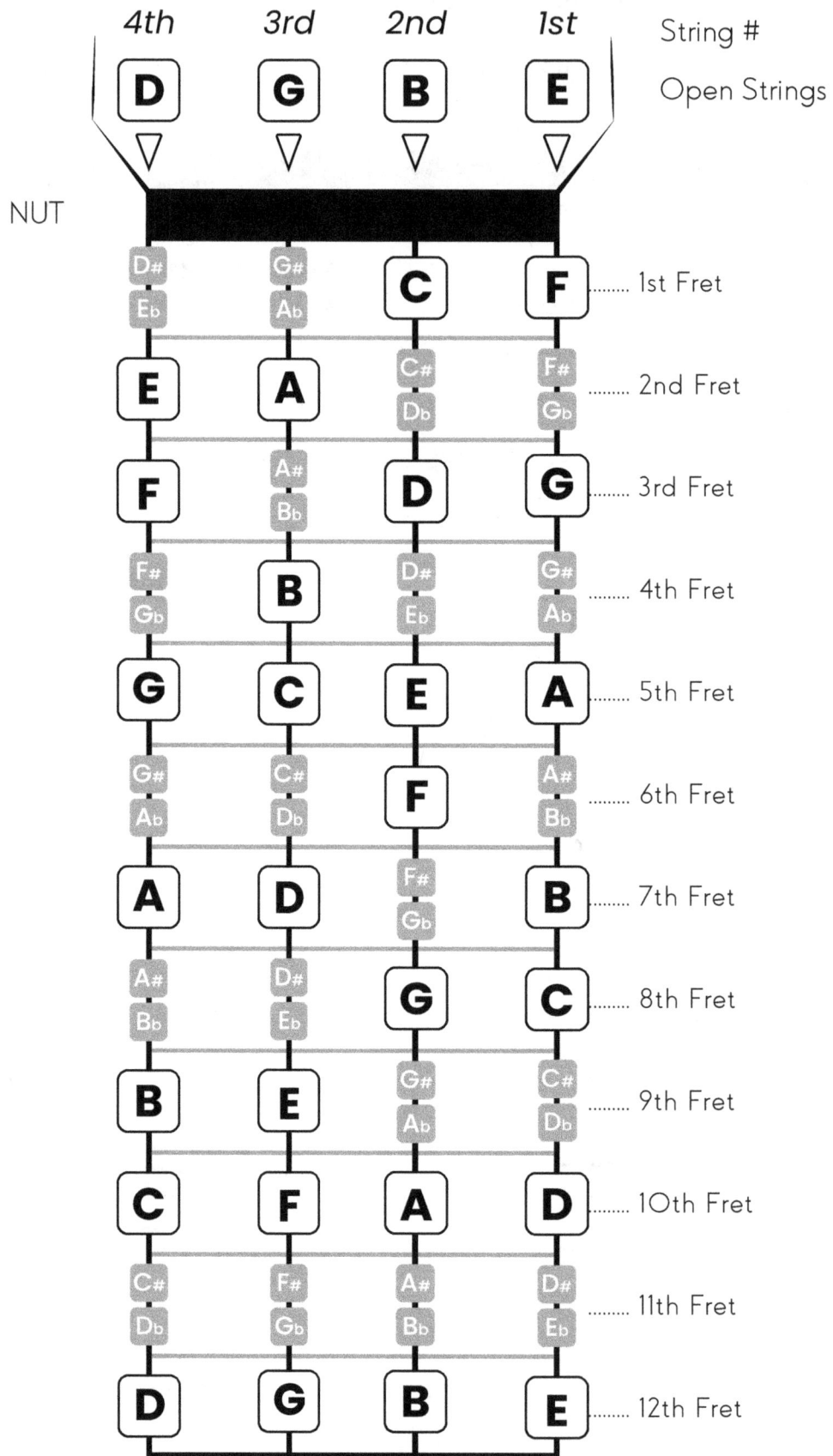

Notes repeat at 12th Fret

E

UNDERSTANDING CHORD DIAGRAMS

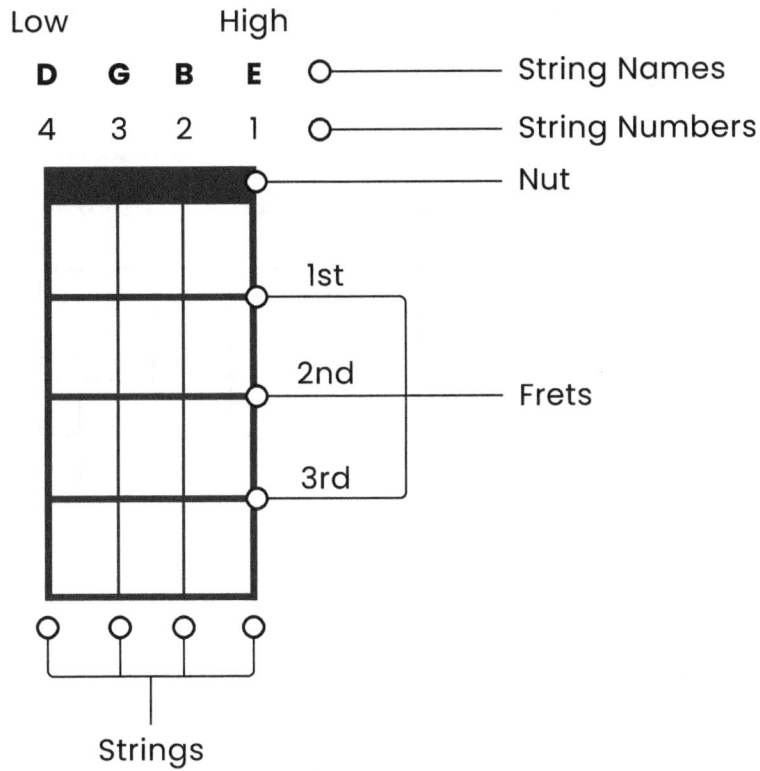

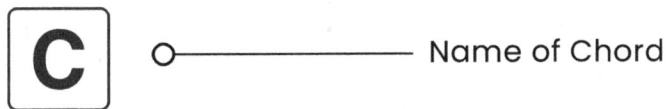

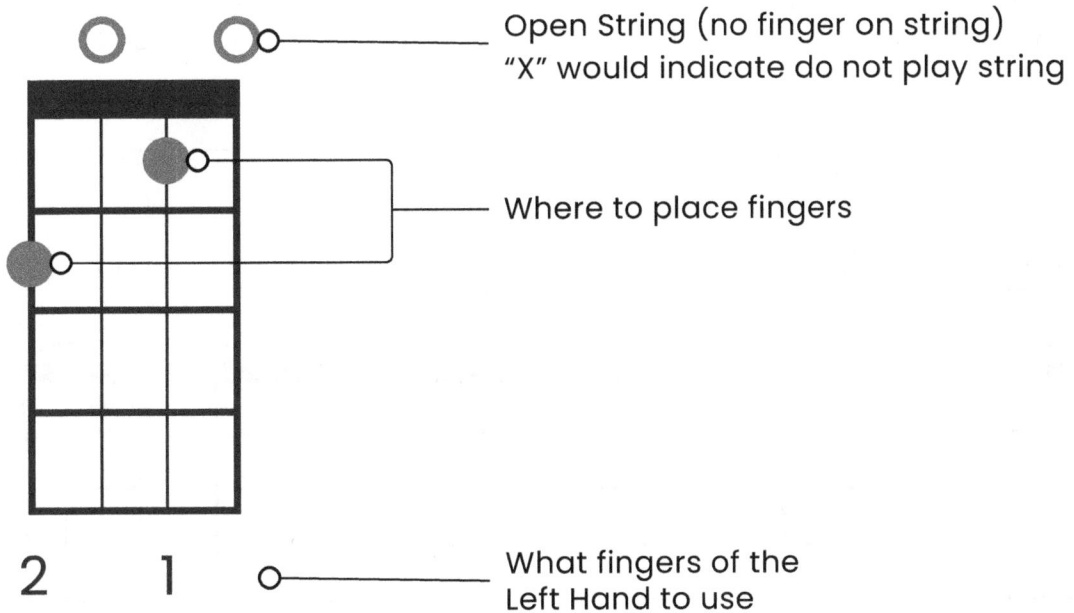

Low   High

D **G** **B** **E** ○——— String Names

4   3   2   1 ○——— String Numbers

○——— Nut

1st

2nd ——— Frets

3rd

○ ○ ○ ○

Strings

C ○——— Name of Chord

○ ○○——— Open String (no finger on string)
"X" would indicate do not play string

——— Where to place fingers

2   1 ○——— What fingers of the
Left Hand to use

BARITONE CHORD CHART

These are some of the most widely used chords in all of music. Although there are more chords than what is listed. these chords represent the most widely used shapes.

MAJOR CHORDS

A	B	C	D	E	F	G
1 1 2	2 2 3 1	2 1	1 3 2	2 1	3 2 1 1	3

MINOR CHORDS

A min	B min	C min	D min	E min	F min	G min
2 3 1	3 4 2 1	3 4 2 1	2 3 1	2	3 1 1 1	3 1 1 1

B min: 2nd FRET
C min: 3rd FRET
G min: 3rd FRET

DOMINANT 7th CHORDS

A⁷	B⁷	C⁷	D⁷	E⁷	F⁷	G⁷
2 3	1 2 3	2 3 1 4	2 1 3	1	1 2 1 1	1

G

MAJOR 7th CHORDS

A_{maj}^{7}	B_{maj}^{7}	C_{maj}^{7}	D_{maj}^{7}	E_{maj}^{7}	F_{maj}^{7}	G_{maj}^{7}

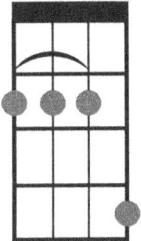
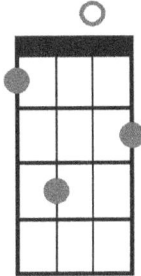
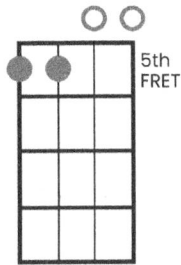
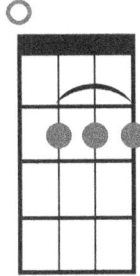
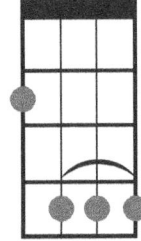
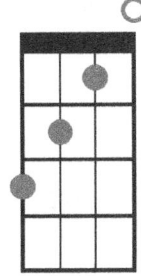
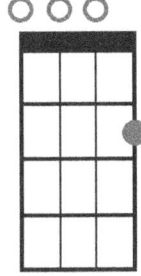

MINOR 7th CHORDS

A_{min}^{7}	B_{min}^{7}	C_{min}^{7}	D_{min}^{7}	E_{min}^{7}	F_{min}^{7}	G_{min}^{7}

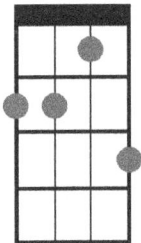
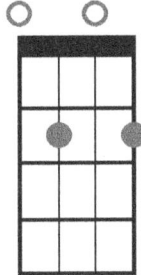
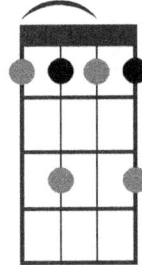
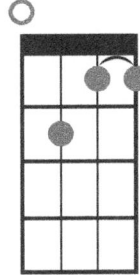
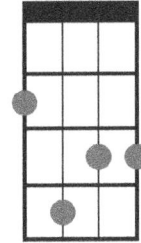
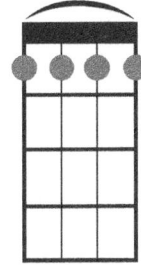
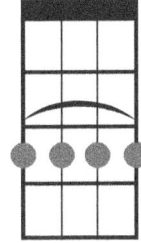

SUS + ADD CHORDS

A_{sus}^{4}	B_{sus}^{4}	C_{add}^{4}	D_{sus}^{4}	E_{sus}^{4}	F_{sus}^{4}	G_{sus}^{4}

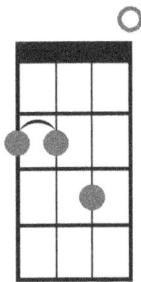
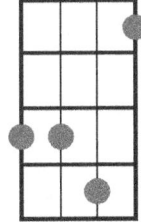
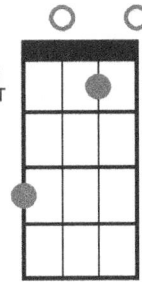
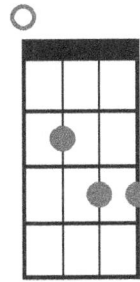
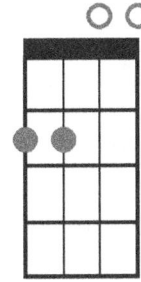
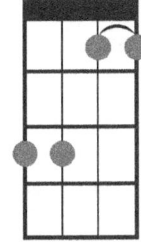
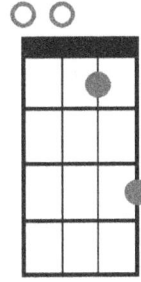

MUSIC SYMBOLS TO KNOW

A variety of symbols, articulations, repeats, hammer on's, pull off's, bends, and slides.

Fermata:
Hold note

Staccato:
Play note short

Accent:
Play note loud

Accented Staccato:
Play note
loud + short

Vibrato
Rapid "shaking"
of note

Arpeggiated Chord:
Play the notes in fast
succession from low
to high strings

Grace Note:
Fast embellishment
note played before
the main note

Mute:
"Muffle" sound of
strings either with
left or right hand

Down Stroke:
Pick string(s) with a
downward motion

Up Stroke:
Pick string(s) with
an upward motion

Tie:
Play first note but
do not play second
note that it is tied to

Ledger Lines:
Extend the staff
higher or lower.

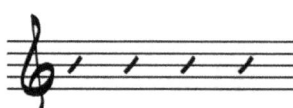

Slash Notation:
Repeat notes & rhythms
from previous measure

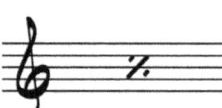

1 Bar Repeat:
Repeat notes &
rhythms from
previous measure

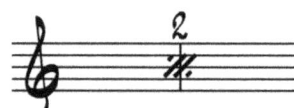

2 Bar Repeat:
Repeat notes & rhythms
from previous 2 measures

Repeat Sign:
(Beginning)

Repeat Sign:
(End)

1st Ending:
Play this part the
first time only

2nd Ending:
Play this part
the second time

(D.C. AL FINE) – *D.C.* (da capo) means go to the beginning of the tune and stop when you get to *Fine*

(D.C. AL CODA) – *D.C.* means go to the beginning of the tune and jump to *Coda* ⊕ when you see the sign ⊕

(D.S. AL FINE) – *D.S.* (dal segno) means go to the *Sign* 𝄋 and stop when you get to *Fine*

(D.S. AL CODA) – *D.S.* means go to the *Sign* 𝄋 And Jump to the *Coda* ⊕ when you see ⊕

SIM... – Play the same rhythm, strum pattern, or picking pattern as the previous measure

ETC... – Continue the same rhythm, strum pattern, or picking pattern as the previous measure

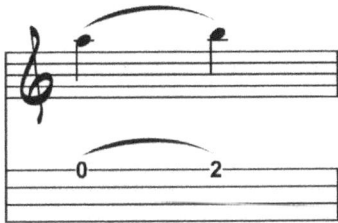

Hammer On:
Pick first note then hammer on to the next note without picking it.

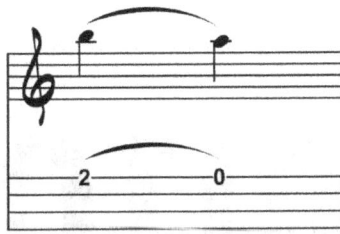

Pull Off:
Pick first note then pull off to the next note without picking it.

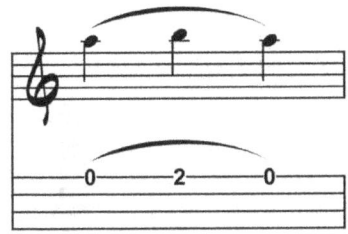

Hammer On & Pull Off:
Pick first note, hammer on to the next note, and pull off to the last note all in one motion.

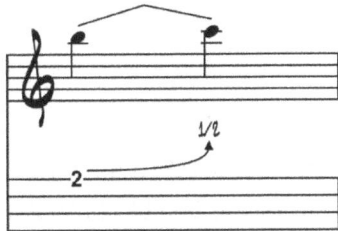

1/2 Step Bend:
Bend the first note a 1/2 step or 1 fret.

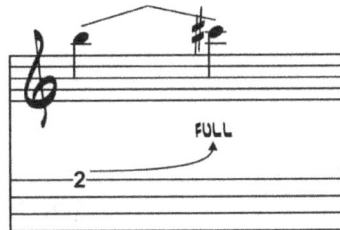

Whole Step Bend:
Bend the first note a whole step or 2 frets.

Step & 1/2 Bend:
Bend the first note 1 1/2 steps or 3 frets.

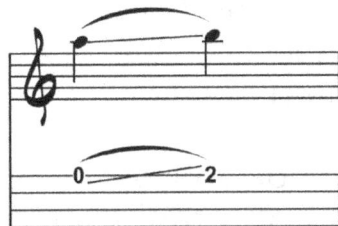

Forward Slide:
Pick first note and slide up to higher note.

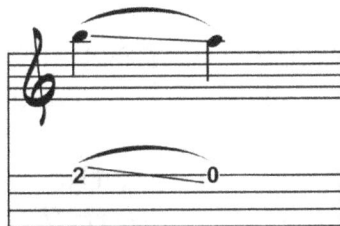

Backward Slide:
Pick first note and slide back to lower note.

Forward/Backward Slide:
Pick first note, slide up to next note and then slide back.

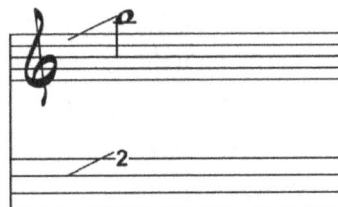

Slide Into Note:
Slide from 2-3 frets below note.

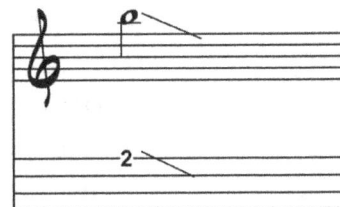

Slide Off Note:
Slide off 2-5 frets after note.

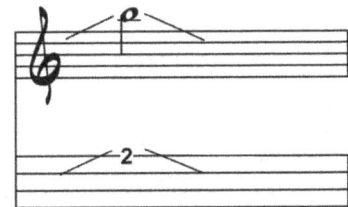

Slide Into Note then Slide Off Note.

BARITONE
UKULELE FINGERSTYLE

Welcome to the **Beginning Baritone Ukulele Fingerstyle Songbook** by Uke Like The Pros and written by Terry Carter. This book is written for the beginning baritone ukulele player who is interested in learning how to finger pick. This book will not only teach you some cool songs, but will also help you develop the fingerstyle techniques necessary to play more advanced fingerstyle pieces. By the end of this book you will also learn and develop 7 of the most important and widely-used fingerstyle patterns, which you can apply to all of your favorite songs.

This Beginning Baritone Ukulele Fingerstyle Songbook is a step-by-step method to master finger picking. Each of the 7 fingerstyle patterns you are going to learn will be introduced in 2 separate lessons. The first lesson will introduce a finger picking pattern and have you practice that pattern over a simple 2-chord progression. This will allow you to focus on learning and memorizing the fingerstyle pattern while not having to worry about switching to a lot of different chords. The second lesson will be an original song

written specifically for you to continue to master the finger picking pattern you just learned. But this time you will apply the pattern over a song that uses more chords, moves around different strings and the fretboard, and sounds cool. These songs will give you a sense of accomplishment when you master them and will make people turn their heads to listen when they hear you playing them.

By the end of this book you will not only learn 7 of the most important fingerpicking patterns, but will have 7 complete songs you can practice and play. As a bonus, at the end of this book, there is a chord progression already written for which you can create your own fingerstyle pattern. Whether you use a pattern that you learn from this book, or you come up with your very own pattern, this will help you develop the skill to apply finger picking to any song.

The Beginning Baritone Ukulele Fingerstyle Songbook will also show you different tips and concepts related to fingerstyle playing, such as the rest stroke vs the free stroke.

This course was written for standard **D – G – B – E** baritone ukulele tuning, and you can use either high D or low D tuning.

With the purchase of this book you will get free access to the slow and fast backing tracks that accompany every lesson at *ukelikethepros.com/baritone-song-book*

There is also a complete video course (sold separately) that is available at: *ukelikethepros.com/baritonefingertyle*

ARE YOU READY?

This is what is needed from you. To make the decision right now that you will stay committed to working on the Beginning Baritone Ukulele Fingerstyle Songbook every day until you get through all the lessons and songs. That means setting aside some time, even if it's just 15 minutes a day, to practice this material.

You will only improve and get better with a daily practice routine and discipline. I realize life it busy with work, families, emergencies and other unexpected things, but decide right now that no matter what, even if you must get up early or go to bed late, that you will practice daily.

The rewards and growth you will see will outweigh any pain or difficulties you might have in keeping up with your practice.

Don't forget to get your free backing tracks for this course at: *ukelikethepros.com/baritone-songbook*

You can post your progress and see how others are doing at the **UKELIKETHEPROS.COM** Forum.

You can also get free access to the backing tracks at: ukelikethepros.com/baritone-songbook

This lesson is a warm-up for "October Rain," and will teach you the fingerstyle pattern **p - i** (**p** =thumb and **i** =index) played over a "G" chord. For measures 1-2 you will play on the 2nd and 3rd open strings, and then move to the 1st and 3rd strings with your 3rd finger on the 3rd fret of the 1st string for measures 3-4 and then repeat. The chords and fingerstyle pattern will prepare you for the song, "October Rain."

Become a **PLATINUM MEMBER** and get access to:

- More than 20 **Online Courses**.
- **LIVE Q&As.**
- Monthly **Challenges and Giveaways**.
- Be part of the **ULTP NATION**, the Best Ukulele Community.
- **VIP Access** For All Challenges and Workshops.
- Find more about this at: **ukelikethepros.com/platinum**

This song uses alternating **p - i** (**p** = thumb and **i** = index) fingerstyle pattern throughout the entire piece. The thumb will play the open 3rd string throughout while the index finger plays the melody, which moves between different frets on strings 1 and 2. Pay attention to the last measure as it has a cool ending lick.

LESSON 03 **REST & FREE STROKE**

This lesson will help you master the 2 common ways to pluck the strings in fingerstyle: The free stroke and the rest stroke. The free stroke is a light and quick stroke that is played with the tip of your finger, and after you pluck the string you will curl your finger into the palm of your hand. The rest stroke is a powerful stroke that also uses your fingertip, but after you pluck the string you will rest your finger on the next adjacent string. This lesson will work on using the thumb, index, and middle finger. For each line start with the rest stroke, and then on the repeat move to a free stroke.

1st time use **Rest Stroke**. Then, use a **Free Stroke** on the repeat.

♩=70

LESSON 04 **COCONUT'S DREAM** WARMUP

This lesson is a warm-up to help you play Coconut's Dream and uses the fingerstyle pattern *p - m - i* (thumb - middle - index). The rhythm is a triplet pattern (3 notes per beat) and can be counted: 1-trip-let, 2-trip-let, 3-trip-let, 4-trip-let. The entire song uses 3 different one-finger "G" major chords.

BIGGEST SELECTION
of Baritones and Guitars
TERRYCARTERMUSICSTORE.COM

LESSON 05 **COCONUT'S DREAM**

This song uses the fingerstyle pattern *p - m - i* (thumb - middle - index). The melody will move from the 2nd string in "A" and "C" section, and to the 4th string in the "B" section. The last 3 chords, G, Gmaj7, and G5 will be played using a downstroke with the thumb. The main rhythm for this song are triplets (3 notes per beat).

Practice Tip:

To develop great timing, always use a metronome or backing tracks when practicing these technique exercises. Sign up for the free backing tracks at **ukelikethepros.com/baritone-songbook**

PLATINUM
MEMBERSHIP

This lesson is a warm-up to help you play "Merry-Go-Round," and uses a backward fingerstyle pattern **m - i - p** (middle, index, and thumb). A backward pattern or backward roll is when you fingerpick from the higher to lower strings. The main rhythm for this song are triplets (3 notes per beat).

You can post your progress and see how others are doing at the **UKELIKETHEPROS.COM** Forum.

You can also get free access to the backing tracks at:
ukelikethepros.com/baritone-songbook

This song uses a backward fingerstyle pattern **m - i - p** (middle, index, and thumb) and a triplet rhythm (3 notes per beat). The "A" and "C" section uses a classic chord progression, G – Emin – C – D7, which is known as the I - vi - IV – V progression. The "B" section focuses on a melody that moves up and down the fretboard.

This lesson is a warm-up to help you play "Catfish Blues," and uses the forward and backward fingerstyle pattern **p - i - m - i** (thumb, middle, index, middle). It uses all 1/8th notes (2 notes per beat) and alternates between the E7 and the A7 chords.

Counting: 1 + 2 + 3 + 4 + Sim...

Picking Hand: p i m i p i m i Sim...

4 Times

m
i
p

PROTECT YOUR BARITONE

LESSON 09 CATFISH BLUES

This blues song uses the fingerstyle pattern **p - i - m - i** (thumb, index, middle, index). It uses all 1/8th notes and uses the E7, A7, and B7 chords (aka as the I, IV, V chords) with some cool blues twists in it. Most traditional blues are 12 measures, but this one has 13 bars and includes a classic blues ending.

LESSON 10 **SONNY'S STROLL** WARMUP

This lesson is a warm-up to help you play "Sonny's Stroll." It is in ¾ time (3 beats per measure) and uses all downstrokes with the thumb for the entire piece. The biggest challenge is controlling the thumb to only play the strings that each chord requires.

WHAT THE STUDENTS SAY:

I absolutely LOVED the baritone fingerstyle course!! Terry Carter has created & presented the lesson content in such a way that you build and improve upon the skills exponentially every lesson. Because Terry has a 360 degree metacognition of playing the instrument, (in addition to understanding how new players comprehend and execute what he's teaching) he can walk you through the fundamentals slowly while increasing the complexity in a way that you'll be amazed that your brain programmed it and soon you can go on auto pilot to play like he can! I guarantee you will be craving to play the patterns again & again. The chords and progressions he has composed for the course are verybeautiful and so pleasing to the ear and to the soul. I go back to play Catfish Blues & October Rain at least once a week just because it makes me feel so good!

Missy Jessen
BARITONE UKULELE
STUDENT.

LESSON 11 **SONNY'S STROLL**

This song is in 3/4 time and only uses the **p** (thumb) for the entire piece. Although the chords are all fairly simple, the trick is controlling the thumb to stop on the indicated string. It seems like there are a lot of chords in this piece, but the focus is how the melody moves between the 1st, 2nd, and 3rd strings.

G
Gmaj7
G
Gmaj7
G
Gmaj7
G
7fr.
Gmaj7
C
G
Gmaj7
G
Gmaj7
G
Gmaj7
Emin7
G
17
Csus2
C
D
G
D
C
G
D

LESSON 12 **SANDY BEACH** WARMUP

This lesson is a warm-up to help you play "Sandy Beach." Besides having a cool name, you will learn the most important fingerpicking pattern, the **p - i - m - a** (thumb, index, middle, ring) pattern. This song is all 1/8th notes and alternates between the G and D7 chords.

ALL ULTP BOOKS

LESSON 13 **SANDY BEACH**

This song uses the ever-important **p - i - m - a** (thumb, index, middle, ring) fingerstyle pattern played over one of the all-time classic progressions, the I - vi - IV - V or G - Emin - C - D7 chords. It is in the key of G Major, uses all 1/8th notes and has a traditional Hawaiian baritone ukulele ending.

This lesson is a warm-up to help you play "Candlelight." It is in the key of D Minor, and uses a bass-pinch pattern that plays the bass note on the 4th string with the thumb, and pinches the chords on strings 1-3 using your index, middle, and ring fingers. Low and High D will work for this one.

Practice Tip:

Practice all these exercises slowly to make sure you play them correctly, accurately, and with the proper fingers. Sign up for the free backing tracks at **ukelikethepros.com/baritone-book.**

Become a **PLATINUM MEMBER** and get access to:

- More than 20 **Online Courses.**
- **LIVE Q&As.**
- Monthly **Challenges and Giveaways.**
- Be part of the **ULTP NATION,** the Best Ukulele Community.
- **VIP Access** For All Challenges and Workshops.
- Find more about this at: **ukelikethepros.com/platinum**

LESSON 15 **CANDLELIGHT**

This song in D Minor uses the bass-pinch fingerstyle pattern where the thumb plays the bass note on the 4th string, while index, middle, and ring fingers pinch strings 1-3. The chords are Dmin – C – Bb – A ,all played with the open 4th string which acts like a drone note over these chords. Low and High D will work for this song.

WRITE YOUR OWN PATTERN

In your final lesson you are going to write your own fingerpicking pattern over the G – E7 – A7 – D7 chord progression. You can use one of the fingerstyle patterns you have already learned, or you can create your own. Fill out the TAB, and if you can, the notation as well. Good Luck!

POST YOUR
WORK

You can post your progress and see how others are doing at the UKELIKETHEPROS.COM Forum.

You can also get free access to the backing tracks at: ukelikethepros.com/baritone-songbook

WHAT THE STUDENTS SAY:

"Are you looking to learn all things ukulele? Are you a beginner, intermediate, or master looking for someone who will get you motivated to try something new or challenge you to become a better player? Then you have come to the right place. Terry Carter and his staff at Uke Like the Pros are the source for all things ukulele. Whether you are in search of a new course or lesson on how to play or are looking for a new ukulele: Baritone, Tenor, Concert, Soprano then this is your one stop shop. Their service is unmatched and I have been very happy with my purchases at ukelikethepros. com. and that's why I am a subscribing member"

Joshua Powers
BARITONE UKULELE
STUDENT.

GREAT
JOB!

Congratulations on completing the Uke Like The Pros Beginning Baritone Ukulele Fingerstyle Songbook. This is an essential book in starting to master fingerstyle on the ukulele. The finger picking patterns and songs in this book have shown you the most important and popular fingerstyle patterns used on the ukulele. Continue to work on these songs and patterns to get smoother and faster playing them. Once you feel confident in these patterns you can apply them to your favorite song and turn any song into a fingerstyle piece.

Did you enjoy the Beginning Baritone Ukulele Fingerstyle Songbook? Wondering what's next?

Here at Uke Like The Pros we take the baritone ukulele very seriously, making sure to help you become the ukulele player that you know you can be. This is why we offer the Platinum Membership. The Platinum Membership gives you access to over 20 online ukulele courses, downloadable TAB, Backing Tracks, and also access to the ULTP Nation. The ULTP Nation is the worldwide community of ukulele players who have dedicated themselves to learning and growing as musicians. With your Platinum Membership you get access to the LIVE Weekly Q & A zoom calls, access to the Member Only Forum, and VIP access to Challenges and Giveaways. You will have the chance to connect with the entire ULTP Nation including the fantastic team here are Uke Like The Pros. Join Uke Like The Pros and let us help you become the ukulele player you know you can be.

I'm proud of you for completing the Beginning Baritone Ukulele Fingerstyle Songbook, and I look forward to connecting with you as a Platinum Member. *ukelikethepros.com/platinum*

Talk soon,
Terry Carter

ABOUT THE AUTHOR

TERRY CARTER

Terry Carter is a San Diego-based ukulele player, surfer, songwriter, and creator of ukelikethepros.com, rocklikethepros.com and terrycartermusicstore.com.

With over 25 years as a professional musician, educator and Los Angeles studio musician, Terry has worked with greats like Weezer, Josh Groban, Robby Krieger (The Doors), 2-time Grammy winning composer Christopher Tin (Calling All Dawns), Duff McKagan (Guns N' Roses), Grammy winning producer Charles Goodan (Santana/Rolling Stones), and the Los Angeles Philharmonic.

Terry has written and produced tracks for commercials (Discount Tire and Puma) and TV shows, including Scorpion (CBS), Pit Bulls & Parolees (Animal Planet), Trippin', Wildboyz, and The Real World (MTV). He has self-published over 10 books for Uke Like The Pros and Rock Like The Pros, filmed over 30 ukulele and guitar online courses and has over 140,000 subscribers on his Uke Like The Pros YouTube channel.

Terry received a Master of Music in Studio/Jazz Guitar Performance from University of Southern California and a Bachelor of Music from San Diego State University, with an emphasis in Jazz Studies and Music Education. He has taught at the University of Southern California, San Diego State University, Santa Monica College, Miracosta College, and Los Angeles Trade Tech College.

TERRY CARTER MUSIC STORE

All your music needs at the #1 music store, **terrycartermusicstore.com**

Baritones

Ukuleles

Guitars

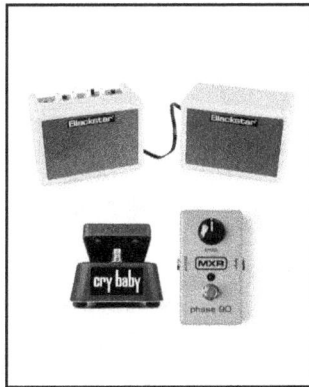

Amplifiers and Pedals

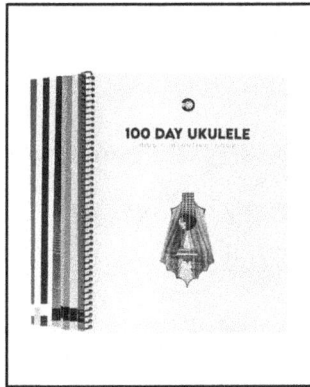

Books

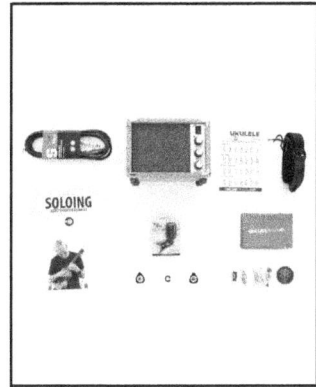

Accessories

ONLINE UKULELE COURSES

The perfect place to learn how to play Ukulele, Baritone Ukulele, Guitar and Guitarlele.

ULTP Roadmap
WHERE TO START?

1) UKULELE BEGINNER
A. Beginning Ukulele Starter Course
B. Beginning Ukulele Bootcamp Course
C. Ukulele Fundamentals Course
D. Ukulele Practice & Technique Course
E. Master the Ukulele 1

2) UKULELE INTERMEDIATE
A. Master The Ukulele 2
B. Beginning Music Reading
C. 23 Ultimate Chord Progressions
D. Beginning Ukulele Fingerstyle Course

3) UKULELE ADVANCED
A. Ukulele Blues Mastery Course
B. Beginning Ukulele Soloing Course
C. Fingerstyle Mastery Course
D. Jazz Swing Mastery Course

MORE OPTIONS!

FUNLAND
A. Beginning Ukulele Kids Course Songbook
B. 21 Popular Songs for Ukulele
C. The Best Ukulele Christmas Songs
D. 10 Classic Rock Licks
E. Guitar Fundamentals

BARITONE UKULELE
A. Beginning Baritone Ukulele Bootcamp Course
B. 6 Weeks Baritone Q&A
C. Baritone Blues Mastery Course
D. Beginning Baritone Fingerstyle Course

GUITARLELE
A. Guitarlele Starter Course
B. 6 Weeks Guitarlele Q&A
C. Guitarlele Course for Ukulele and Guitar Players
D. Guitarlele Blues Mastery Course

PLATINUM MEMBERSHIP: VIP ACCESS TO ALL COURSES, CHALLENGES, WORKSHOPS, GIVEAWAYS AND Q&AS!

BARITONE UKULELE STEP IT UP!

UKULELE Advanced BECOME A PRO!

FUNLAND SONGS AND MORE SONGS!

UKULELE Intermediate KEEP ROCKING!

GUITARLELE 6 STRINGS FUN! For Ukulele & Guitar Players

UKULELE Beginner

START HERE! Welcome

GUITARLELE BLUES MASTERY COURSE

UKULELE MUSIC READING COURSE

23 ULTIMATE CHORD PROGRESSIONS COURSE

GUITARLELE FOR UKULELE & GUITAR PLAYERS COURSE

BEGINNING UKULELE SOLOING COURSE

CHRISTMAS SONGS FOR UKULELE COURSE

BEGINNING UKULELE BOOTCAMP COURSE

BEGINNING BARITONE UKULELE BOOTCAMP

BEGINNING UKULELE STARTER COURSE

21 POPULAR SONGS FOR UKULELE

BEGINNING BARITONE FINGERSTYLE COURSE

INTERMEDIATE MASTER THE UKULELE #2 COURSE

BEGINNING PRACTICE & TECHNIQUE BOOTCAMP

UKULELE FINGERSTYLE COURSE

BEGINNING UKULELE FINGERSTYLE COURSE

UKULELE BLUES MASTERY COURSE

BARITONE BLUES MASTERY COURSE

BEGINNING MASTER THE UKULELE #1 COURSE

JAZZ SWING MASTERY #1 COURSE

KIDS UKULELE COURSE

Courses For All Levels
UKELIKETHEPROS.COM

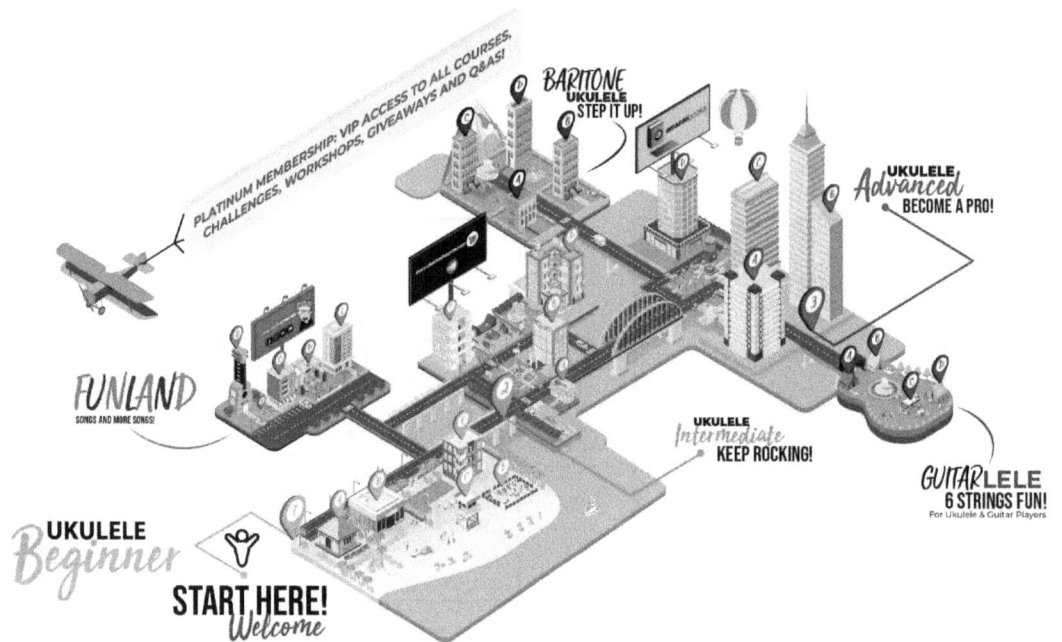

UKELIKETHEPROS.COM
BLOG.UKELIKETHEPROS.COM
TERRYCARTERMUSICSTORE.COM

@ukelikethepros

INTERESTED IN **GUITAR** CONTENT?
ROCKLIKETHEPROS.COM

www.ingramcontent.com/pod-product-compliance
Lightning Source LLC
Chambersburg PA
CBHW081242090426
42738CB00016B/3378